CH00392741

Short *ish*
Torbay and Dartmouth

Paul White

Bossiney Books

This second edition published 2017 by
Bossiney Books Ltd, 33 Queens Drive, Ilkley, LS29 9QW
First published 2006
www.bossineybooks.com

ISBN 978-1-906474-62-1

Acknowledgements
The author and publishers are grateful to Robert Hesketh for his work in the
preparation of this new edition. The maps are by Graham Hallowell.
The photographs are by Robert Hesketh.
Cover based on a design by Heards Design Partnership. The boots
were kindly supplied by The Brasher Boot Company.

Printed in Great Britain by R Booth Ltd, Penryn, Cornwall

All the walks in this book were checked prior to publication,
at which time the instructions were correct. However, changes can occur
over which neither the author nor publisher has any control. Please let
us know if you encounter any serious problems.

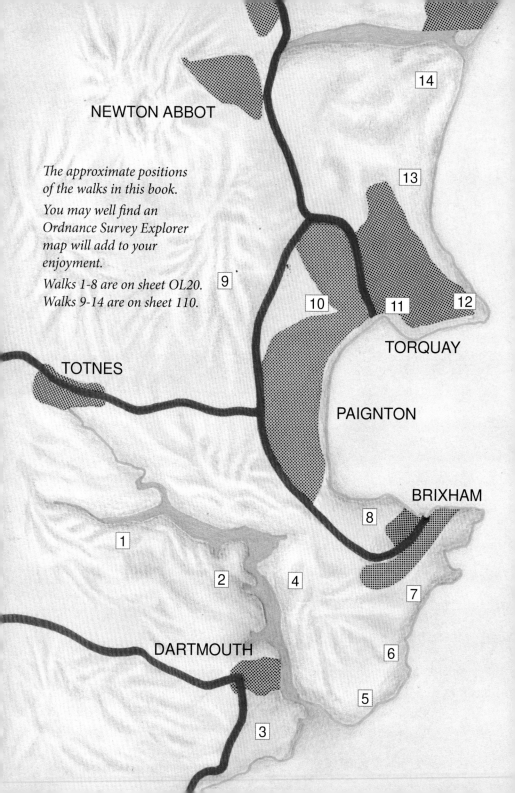

NEWTON ABBOT

The approximate positions of the walks in this book.

You may well find an Ordnance Survey Explorer map will add to your enjoyment.

Walks 1-8 are on sheet OL20. Walks 9-14 are on sheet 110.

14

13

9

10

11

12

TORQUAY

TOTNES

PAIGNTON

BRIXHAM

8

1

2

4

7

6

DARTMOUTH

5

3

Introduction

This is a book of mainly rural walks in one of Devon's loveliest coastal areas, though a couple of walks are devoted to the delights of Cockington and of Torquay itself, and are part urban.

The walks vary in length from 4.1 to 8.7 km (2 3/4 to 5 1/2 miles) and will each occupy two or three hours. We give approximate times for each walk but exactly how long you take will depend on many factors: there are plenty of distractions, from birdwatching and beaches to shopping in Dartmouth, not to mention pubs and cream teas.

But the time you take will also depend on your fitness, because whilst these walks are 'shortish' by the standards of regular walkers, some of them are quite strenuous. Torquay and the surrounding area flourished as a place for invalids because of its famously mild microclimate, but its gradients seem ideally designed to kill them off. As on any rural walk, you will encounter stiles, but most of them in this area are well maintained.

Access

At the height of the season the traffic can make both driving and parking rather tiresome, but many of the walks in this book can be reached by public transport. In addition to buses, you can from March to October use the steam train from Paignton to Churston and Kingswear (for Dartmouth), or the ferry services from Dartmouth to Dittisham, Brixham to Dartmouth, and Dittisham to Greenway Quay.

Comfort and safety

Country walking involves some mud at most times of the year and in winter, or after summer rain, a lot of mud! I recommend walking boots for the majority of these walks, not just for the mud but to give ankle support on the cliff path sections. I also find a walking pole or stick invaluable when descending the steeper bits of the coast path.

Cliff paths are exposed to the wind, so you may find you need an extra layer or two, as well as a waterproof. As you will be walking for some time, it is sensible to carry water and perhaps a snack.

The most obvious hazards are the cliff paths, which are unfenced so children and dogs need to be supervised, and traffic. In Bossiney Walks Books we try to avoid roads wherever we can, but in a populous area like this it has not always been possible, so take care. I hope you will enjoy these walks as much as I have.

Paul White

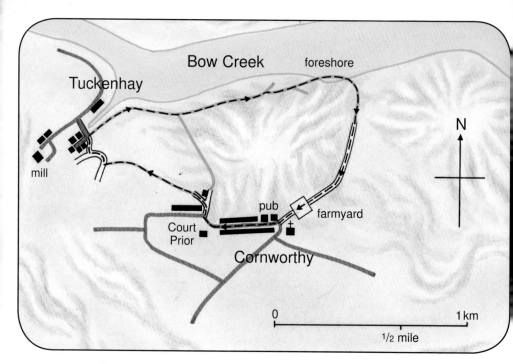

Walk 1   Cornworthy and Tuckenhay

Distance: 4.1km (2¹/₂ miles)   Time: 1¹/₂ hours
Character: A walk between two interesting villages, Cornworthy, an
archetypal Devon settlement with church, pub and thatched cottages,
and Tuckenhay, an industrial hamlet founded by one Abraham Tucker
on a tidal creek.

Two paper mills and a corn mill made it a thriving place throughout
the 19th century. Road access was then less important than river trans-
port. The villages are connected by an ancient trackway, and the return
path is alongside tidal Bow Creek. Avoid the three hours surrounding
high tide, as part of the walk is along a tidal foreshore.

Park somewhere downhill from the Hunter's Lodge pub in Cornworthy's village street, trying not to inconvenience the residents. Walk
downhill to Court Prior: there was a priory of Augustinian nuns just
west of the village during the middle ages, of which only a gatehouse
survives.

Turn right (UNMETALLED ROAD) between cottages, then keep left up
an old track.

In the earliest detailed map of Devon's roads (1765) this is shown as
the main road into the village, and it is quite typical of Devon roads of

4

that period, before turnpike trusts took over. Nowadays it's a footpath between high hedges.

Ignore a stile on the right with a footpath sign – it's a short cut, but rather steep. Turn sharp right at a T-junction, then sharp right again at the next junction. When the track joins a residential street, you will ultimately need to turn right (PUBLIC FOOTPATH). However, you will probably want to walk down to the road junction and explore a little way in either direction, and admire Tuckenhay Mill with its clock tower, before returning to this point.

Take the PUBLIC FOOTPATH along the creekside and through a kissing gate. After about 350m you will see a waymark on the left (DART VALLEY TRAIL). Follow this lesser path down and at a junction turn left for the TIDAL ROUTE.

At a fork, bear right, then keep left downhill at the next junction, which brings you down to a brief stretch of tidal shoreline.

Leave the 'beach' by a stile and cross the field ahead. The path then turns right (waymarked). Walk up the field with the hedge on your left. Join a track which leads steadily upwards to a farmyard. Go through the farmyard then bear left, and you will find yourself at Cornworthy church. Turn right here back past the pub to your car.

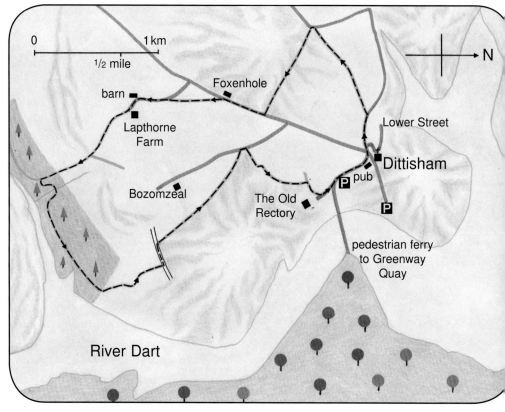

Walk 2 Dittisham

Distance: 8.5km (5¹/₄ miles)   Time: 3¹/₄ hours
*Character: A superb rural walk with varied and lovely scenery – views
over the River Dart, tidal creeks, stretches of woodland and open
farmland. But the views come at a price: there are four steep and/or
prolonged ascents.*

Dittisham is a delightful village, with two car parks and some on-road
parking. The walk starts from the cross-roads by the church and pub
(SX 861551). Take the COOMBE road.

After 300m, at the top of a slope, turn left up PUBLIC FOOTPATH.
Climb then descend, keeping the hedge on your left, then follow
the sign onward across a field. Go through the gate into a lane, then
immediately turn left up a track, UNMETALLED ROAD.

Reaching a lane, turn right. Take care, as this is the main access to
Dittisham and can be quite busy. After 350m, opposite 'Foxenhole',
turn left (PUBLIC FOOTPATH) and cut diagonally across two fields to a

6

lane. Turn left and follow it down to a barn. Ignore the footpath to the right. Keep left on the track, then bear right along LAPTHORNE LANE.

Ignore a PUBLIC BRIDLEWAY to the left and a gated track. Continue to a fingerpost, and turn left onto PERMISSIVE FOOTPATH DITTISHAM. For the rest of the walk follow the blue DART VALLEY TRAIL signs, first through woodland, then uphill onto farmland. Notice on your left the restored manor house of Bozomzeal, nestling in its cleave. At a summit field, keep left along a track.

Ultimately you will reach a lane. Turn right, DITTISHAM, then after 100 m turn right (PUBLIC FOOTPATH) and follow this downhill, with a superb view ahead. Reaching a track, turn right down it, cross a stile, then bear left away from 'The Old Rectory'.

We tend now to have forgotten the old distinctions between clergy: a rector owned the tithes of the village, and could be a wealthy man. He might employ a curate, on a low wage, to carry out his duties and himself live elsewhere, or he could live like a squire in a rather nice house like this one. A vicar was in charge of a parish where the tithes had been appropriated, for example to fund an Oxbridge college.

Follow the lane. Keep left at a junction, pass a car park, and continue to the Red Lion and church. The cottages in Lower Street, downhill from the church, are well worth a detour.

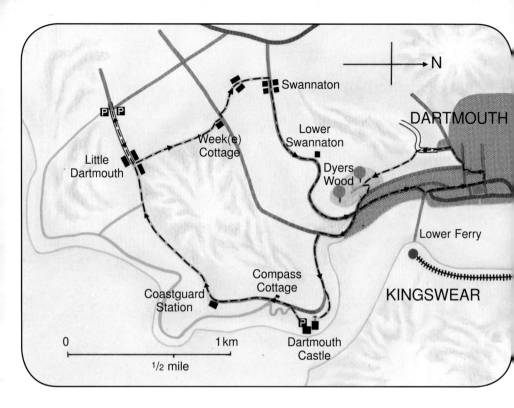

Walk 3   Dartmouth

Distance: 7.2km (4½ miles)   Time: 2 hours
Character: If you don't already know Dartmouth, this walk will give
you a taster. It provides dramatic views over the estuary – but that
means climbing hills! The section over Dyer's Hill could be omitted,
leaving just one prolonged ascent of about 120m (400ft). There is one
lengthy section of quiet lane, as well as town streets with pavements.

You could start from the town and walk out, but I started from the
National Trust car park at Little Dartmouth (SX874491). Take the
PUBLIC BRIDLEWAY TO JUBILEE WAY to Little Dartmouth Farm. Walk
through the yard, then turn left, signed WEEKE COTTAGE. Skirt to the
left of the cottage and turn left up the lane. After 50m turn right,
PUBLIC FOOTPATH SWANNATON. When the track forks, keep left then
right (waymarked); pass to the left of a barn conversion, then follow
a mud track uphill to a lane. Turn right.

 Swannaton Lane is very narrow, and little used, but you still need
to take care. It leads down to Dartmouth – and a superb view of the
town opens up. Keep left along SOUTH TOWN, and after 500m bear

8

right down pedestrianised BAYARDS HILL. After a look at Bayards Cove to your right, turn left and continue ahead till you reach the inner harbour and the Castle Hotel. Turn left, passing the magnificent Butterwalk, then left again up ANZAC STREET to pass the church.

The next section is a very steep detour, which you can avoid by returning the way you came, and rejoining us at the foot of Swannaton Road. But if you've got lots of energy, climb the steps ahead of you and turn right, then immediately left. Climb CROWTHER HILL (steep) then take the second left into JAWBONES HILL (steeper). It becomes a track. At a bend, go through a kissing gate and follow the uppermost footpath (DYERS WOOD) and keep left at a bench.

Within the wood, go through a gate and descend a few steps, then turn left down a longer flight. Zig-zag down to a lane and turn right. This descends steeply. Continue down WARFLEET ROAD, then turn left into CASTLE ROAD. At a fork, follow the COAST PATH waymarks which lead past the castle and its church. From the castle car park, take COAST PATH STOKE FLEMING and climb the steps to a lane and turn left.

The coast path itself is very beautiful but has numerous taxing flights of steps. Instead, I suggest you keep right (ACCESS TO COMPASS COVE COTTAGE). Keep right again at the cottage, then at the Coastguard Station follow the PUBLIC BRIDLEWAY which leads back to Little Dartmouth Farm.

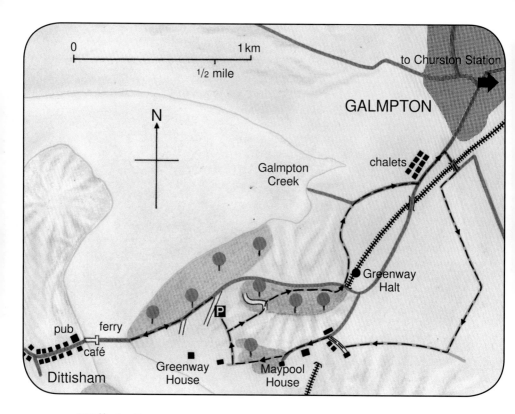

Walk 4 Greenway

Distance: 6 km (3 1/2 miles)   Time: 1 3/4 hours
Character: Lovely woodland, views over the Dart estuary, pleasant
footpaths and lanes. Some hills. The walk could be combined with a
visit to the Greenway gardens (National Trust): please note that the car
park at Greenway is for visitors to the gardens only.
Access: Whilst it would be possible to park at Galmpton, in the season
it may be more fun to take a steam train to Greenway Halt (see sketch
map). Or do as I did and take the frequent ferry across from Dittisham,
where there are two pubs and a café. (Last ferry 5pm. Ferry information
01803 844010, www.greenwayferry.com)
For most of the year, a boat plies regularly between Dartmouth and
Dittisham, so you could start with a river trip from Dartmouth.

From the Greenway ferry, walk up the lane, ignoring a pedestrian
entrance to Greenway, to the main entrance into the National Trust
property. Turn sharp right (GREENWAY GARDENS AND KINGSWEAR),
then left into the car park. Leave the car park by the field gate, STEEP

PEDESTRIAN ROUTE TO GREENWAY HALT.

Ascend the hill and enjoy the view. Turn left on GALMPTON VILLAGE WALK. The path leads to a field; keep near the left hedge and then down a track and through a wooden gate (GREENWAY WALK). After 70 m, continue ahead on a footpath. Keep right on PERMISSIVE PATH GALMPTON. Emerging from the wood, cross a lane (PERMISSIVE PATH GALMPTON).

(If you are starting from Greenway Halt, walk up the ramp from the platform and join the route at this point.)

Descend the field to a waymark, then to a gate into a path. Meeting a narrow lane, continue ahead for GALMPTON. After passing chalets on the left, turn right into KENNEL LANE.

Cross the railway and turn right on COMBE LANE PUBLIC BRIDLEWAY. At a T-junction turn right, then at the next junction bear right (GREENWAY WALK). Turn left along the lane (MAYPOOL etc). Continue ahead on the footpath past the Youth Hostel and enter National Trust land. Where a bench provides a superb view of the river, turn right (GREENWAY GARDENS) and head uphill with woodland on your right.

At the end of the field, if you started at the ferry turn left and retrace your steps. If you started at Galmpton, turn right.

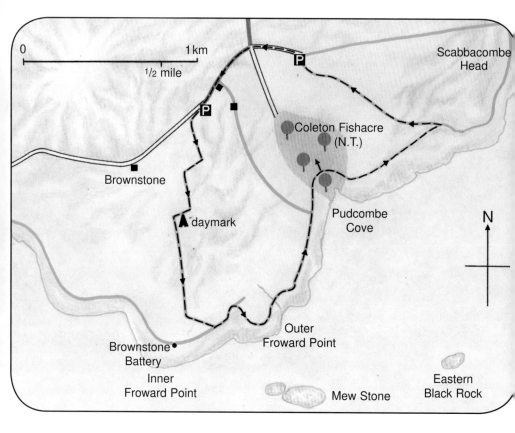

Walk 5 Coleton Fishacre and Froward Point

Distance: 5.8 km (3 1/2 miles)   Time: 1 3/4 hours
Character: A glorious stretch of coast path, which involves some
fairly steep ascents and descents. Can be combined with a visit to the
National Trust's beautiful garden at Coleton Fishacre.

Start from the Coleton Camp car park (SX910512), which is reached
by turning left along a track from the entrance to the National Trust
property. Walk back along the track, then continue past Coleton
Barton Farm and into the Higher Brownstone car park.

Follow the track from the gate in the car park. At a junction, turn
left (COASTAL FOOTPATH) and follow the track round the daymark
then down towards the sea. Turn left onto LINK TO COAST PATH and
then at the yellow waymark continue ahead. Follow the yellow waymarks as the coast path wiggles, dips and climbs, with views of the
Mew Stone offshore.

Ignore a path on the left back to the car parks, and go through a gate into the Coleton Fishacre woods. At the next two junctions, turn right, unless you want to visit the property; as a noticeboard explains, you may enter this way, but need to obtain a ticket or show your membership card at the main entrance.

The coast path emerges from the woods. At a junction, turn left for COLETON CAMP CAR PARK. Once over the stile, cross the field towards a pair of trees. Then follow the track up the side of a field. Near a phone mast, cross a track and go through the kissing gate into the car park.

Brownstone Battery
A short diversion is possible (see map) to this substantial WW2 survival, which was built to defend Dartmouth. It was manned by 230 men from the Bedfordshire Yeomanry Regiment. Now there are interpretation boards and a Coastwatch post, with friendly staff.

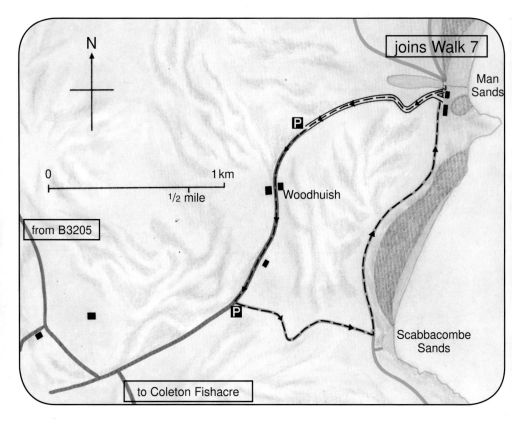

Walk 6   Scabbacombe Sands

Distance: 4.5 km (2³/₄ miles)   Time: 1¹/₂ hours
Character: A walk where Devon's rolling hills meet the sea, visiting two
beautiful coves with beaches. Although this is a short walk, there are
two steep ascents, one of them very steep, the other prolonged, and two
steep grassy descents which could be tricky after rain.

This walk could be combined with Walk 7.

The freshwater lake at Man Sands attracts water birds, particularly
since the National Trust deliberately removed some sea defences to
allow nature to take its course: this beach will be liable to change as sea
levels rise, and could be changed by a single major storm.

The beach at Scabbacombe is sometimes used by nudists.

Park at Woodhuish car park. To get there, follow signs from the B3205
for Coleton Fishacre. When the road turns left then right, take the left
turn then continue ahead signed to CAR PARKS SCABBACOMBE AND
MAN SANDS. The car park is on the right after 900 m (¹/₂ mile).

14

From the car park, take the footpath signed SCABBACOMBE SANDS. At the foot of the valley, turn left on the COASTAL FOOTPATH. But what comes down must go up! And then vice versa – descend steeply to Man Sands, with its lake and ruined lime kiln. Turn left along the track, then right to enjoy the beach.

Leave the beach by the track which runs to the left of the lake and winds inland up the valley. You will pass a car park, then a farm, then more farm buildings before finally, at the very top of the hill, reaching the car park from which you started.

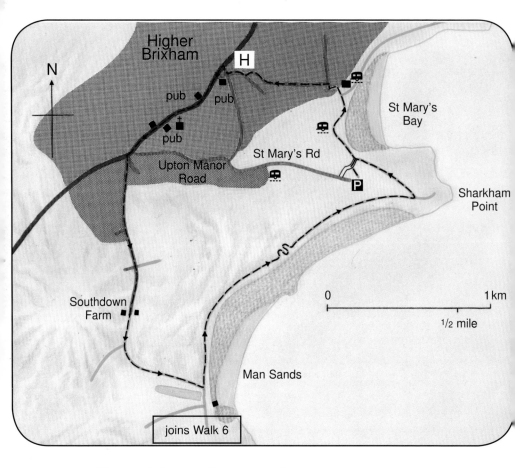

N

Higher Brixham

H

pub

pub

pub

St Mary's Bay

St Mary's Rd

Upton Manor Road

P

Sharkham Point

0   1 km

1/2 mile

Southdown Farm

Man Sands

joins Walk 6

Walk 7   Brixham and Man Sands

Distance: 6.5 km (4 miles)   Time: 2 hours
Character: A strenuous but rewarding walk, first exploring what was
once the agricultural village of Higher Brixham ('cow town' as opposed
to 'fish town'), then following an old lane to an unusual and attractive
beach before returning by the cliff path. Several steep ascents, one of
them very steep. This walk could be combined with Walk 6.

You could take public transport and start from the church in Higher
Brixham. If going by car, use the Sharkham Point free car park
(SX 932547) at the end of St Mary's Road. Take one of the yellow
waymarked paths on the north side which will bring you down to St
Mary's Bay.

Join the coast path, going straight on in the direction of BERRY

16

HEAD. Steps lead the path around the back of the bay past holiday chalets. Reaching buildings ahead of you, go across the low stile and after 20m turn left, then right into Mudstone Lane, and first left into Penn Meadows.

Keep left at the hospital, then turn right at a T-junction. Descend to a crossroads. Turn right and after 100m left, noting the early nineteenth century villa ahead of you – one of several similar which, along with the church, Tudor farmhouses and the former manor house called Black House, add to the interest of this ancient village, even if it has been swallowed by modern development.

Follow the main street (Drew Street) past pubs and the church. (Horsepool Street to the right contains three old farmhouses.) Some 400m beyond the church, opposite a three-storey thatched house, turn left and climb SOUTHDOWN HILL ROAD. Ignore side turnings and at Southdown Farm continue by the footpath ahead, SOUTHDOWN LANE MANSANDS. At a junction, keep left on MANSANDS LANE down to the beach. (See Walk 6 for a description.)

Take a breather here, before turning north up the coast path – very steep to start with. Follow it to the nature reserve on Sharkham Point, then around the point and back to the track by which you started. Turn left for the car park, or right if you started at Brixham.

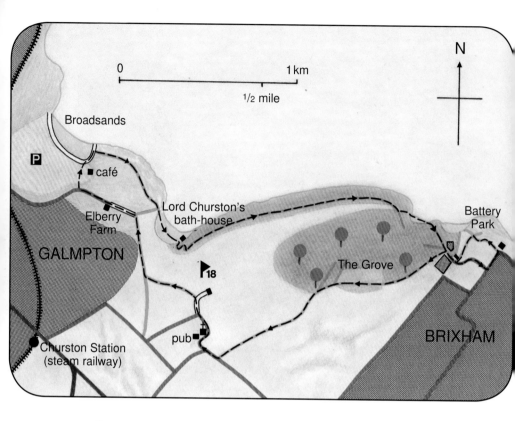

Walk 8   Churston Ferrers

Distance for the circuit: 5 km (3 miles)   Time: 1 1/2 hours
(If you start from Battery Park, add another 0.8 km, 1/2 mile.)
Character: A surprisingly rural walk to find so close to Brixham and
Goodrington, much of it in woodland, with a stretch of coastal path –
and its inevitable ascents and descents. (The woodland known as The
Grove also provides attractive walking but, as I have found, it is very
easy to get lost on its complex of paths!)

   There are several possible starting points: the extensive Broadsands
beach car park at Goodrington, the pub and church at Churston
Ferrers (on road parking) or you could start as I did from Battery Park
at the northern tip of Brixham (SX 921569), also with on road parking.

From the WW2 gunnery observation post, walk down the main path,
go through a pointed arch and after 50 m turn left. Reaching a lane,
turn right past the Holiday Park and continue on PUBLIC FOOTPATH
TO CHURSTON FERRERS.

18

Go through a gate and turn left, GREENWAY VIA CHURSTON FERRERS. This is where the circuit proper begins. The path leads gently uphill, then up a few steps.

At path junctions, follow CHURSTON FERRERS. At a lane, turn right and shortly bear right towards Churston Court, a Grade 1 listed inn, and the church. Follow the lane around the church and up a slope. At the top, continue on the private road for BROADSANDS, and then on the path ELBERRY COVE. This leads briefly across a golf course then along a path.

Ignore the first path on your right. Only a few metres ahead, turn right down a second path. After 300 m, turn left at a path junction and walk past Elberry Farm.

Turn right to the beach, pass the beach huts, then right again along the coast path. This soon takes you across the pebbles at the back of Elberry Cove. The ruin was apparently once Lord Churston's bath-house, where he used to take a hot bath followed by a cold plunge.

The path climbs steeply up the cliff, followed by a level wooded stretch beside the golf course. Shortly after a notice board welcoming you to The Grove, turn left and soon descend steps to a cove: cross it and continue towards Brixham and uphill, keeping left to a finger-post. Turn left for Battery Park, or continue for CHURSTON FERRERS if you started elsewhere.

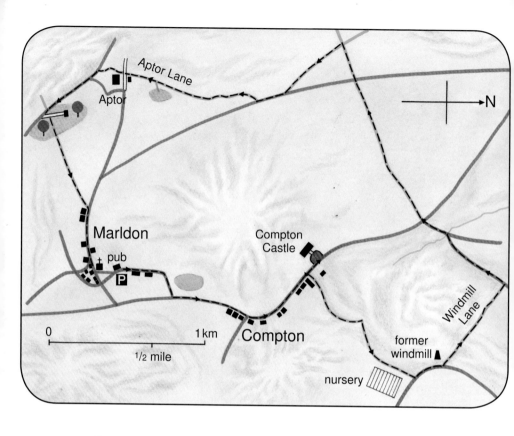

Walk 9   Marldon and Compton Castle

Distance: 8.7 km (5 1/2 miles)   Time: 2 1/2 hours
Character: Almost totally a rural walk, through archetypal Devon
hills and red earth scenery. Mostly on footpaths and byways, but with
some quiet lanes, and one busier section at the start through Compton
village. Likely to be muddy in places. Two sharp ascents.

Start from the public car park opposite the Church House pub in
Marldon (SX 867636). Facing the pub, turn right down a lane; keep
right to arrive at a T-junction. Turn left. The next stretch can be busy,
especially in summer, so take great care.

Walk as far as the front of the castle – National Trust, seasonal
opening, and well worth visiting either now or on another occasion
when you have clean shoes, since it's inhabited! Now retrace your
steps for 100 m and turn left up PUBLIC FOOTPATH. Climb steeply, but
take a look back at the view of the castle. Cross three stiles and follow
the left edge of a field to a PUBLIC FOOTPATH sign. Cut across the field

as directed, to another stile, then continue in the same direction along a track past an extensive nursery.

Reaching a lane, turn left and after 200 m bear left along WINDMILL LANE (a byway). At the end, turn left onto a lane. Ignore side turnings and continue to a T-junction. Go straight ahead on another track, UNMETALLED ROAD.

Cross a tarmac lane into TANYARD LANE. After 250 m turn left (PUBLIC BRIDLEWAY) and follow this to a tarmac lane. Turn right and after 300 m right again onto APTOR LANE. Reaching a junction of tracks at a farm, go straight ahead on PUBLIC BRIDLEWAY and descend to a lane.

Turn left along the lane and ignore the left turn. After 350 m, turn left across a driveway and up a PUBLIC FOOTPATH, climbing steps through a wood to a kissing gate. Now follow the waymarks and well beaten path, until you emerge on a lane.

Turn right along the lane and then bear left down CHURCH HILL which is a 25% gradient, so the sign tells us, but it may feel steeper! Just past the church, turn left opposite 'Old School House', back to the car park – and perhaps the pub.

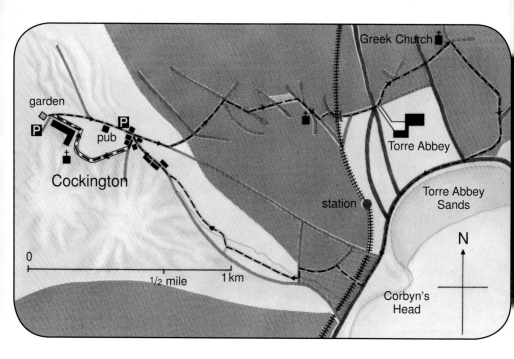

Walk 10 Cockington

Distance: 6 km (3³/₄ miles)   Time: 1¹/₂ hours
Character: A very traditional Torquay walk to the deliberately
picturesque village of Cockington, and the delightful grounds of its
Court, then an exploration of some lesser known parts of Torquay,
including its historic nucleus. For a fuller understanding of what you
are seeing, see Torbay, the Visible History *by Jack Whitton (Bossiney*
Books). Easy walking, much of it on tarmac.

Start from the sea front at Torre Abbey Sands. (Alternatively you
could start from Cockington.) Walk away from Torquay harbour, past
the Grand Hotel and Corbyn's Head. Shortly after passing Seaway
Lane, turn right on PUBLIC FOOTPATH HENNAPYN ROAD. Reaching the
road, turn left. At a T-junction, turn left then almost immediately
right onto a footpath (COCKINGTON).

Follow the path up the valley, parallel to Cockington Lane, which
you ultimately have to join. Continue to the village crossroads, and
turn left at the forge, pass 'Weavers Cottage', then bear right (COCKING-
TON COURT, CHURCH & CAFE). Follow the drive up to the church, pass
across the front of the Court and turn left up the side as far as the
walled organic garden.

Returning from the garden, bear left up a narrow lane. Pass the Drum Inn (designed by Lutyens) and descend to the car park and crossroads. At the Old School House, keep left and continue up the lane, ignoring side turnings. At a junction, continue ahead by a grassy triangle into HERBERT ROAD. At the next junction turn right down HUXTABLE HILL.

At a fork, bear left to pass 'Penrice'. Cross a road and take the path down steps. Continue downhill on a road, turn right past the church, then left into ROUSDOWN ROAD and immediately sharp left, PUBLIC FOOTPATH GOSHEN ROAD, then on under the railway bridge. Turn left (TOWN CENTRE) to arrive at traffic lights.

To cut the walk short, take the right turn into the grounds of Torre Abbey, and make your way back to the sea front.

Alternatively, for an interesting but rather unscenic diversion, cross at the traffic lights, then turn left up FALKLAND ROAD. Keep right at Nethway Hotel, and go forward at the traffic lights which will bring you to Tor Church, at the heart of the medieval village but heavily restored by the Victorians and now a Greek Orthodox church.

Walk a few metres up ST ELFRIDE'S ROAD to see a building which has escaped from ancient Rome! It once supported the terraced garden of Lauriston House, which occupied the top of the original 'tor'.

Return and take CROFT ROAD. At its end, turn right down SHEDDEN HILL which will bring you back to the sea front.

23

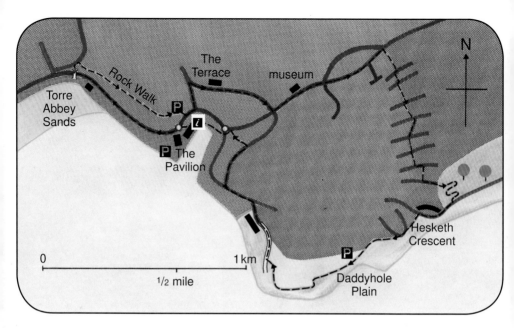

Walk 11   A Torquay history walk

Distance: 6km (3³/4 miles)   Time: 1³/4 hours
Character: An urban walk, but with some surprisingly rural aspects. It
will show you some of Torquay's best early nineteenth century
architecture, built when it took over from Bath as 'Society's' pleasure
capital. There are some very stiff climbs, involving steps.

Start from The Pavilion, not far from the Tourist Information Centre
and the harbour. Walk away from the harbour, past the Torbay Hotel
then the Princess Theatre. Cross the road by a pedestrian footbridge,
turn right up Shedden Hill, and then right again into ROCK WALK,
which leads back along the edge of the cliff.

   Steps lead you down to the main road. Turn left across the entrance
to a multi-storey car park, then left again up semi-pedestrianised Fleet
Street. Try to imagine it 250 years ago, as a picturesque and unspoilt
stream with a mill! After 100m turn sharp right up a narrower semi-
pedestrianised street, with St John's church high above you on your
left. Pass Hagley House and The Terrace.

   At the traffic lights, turn left and climb gently past the museum and
around an S-bend. Notice the luxurious early Victorian developments
in the valley. About 100m after passing LISBURNE SQUARE turn right
into a path opposite OLD TORWOOD ROAD, and start a serious climb.

   Cross three roads (in each case right and immediately left) and at

24

the fourth (the summit!) bear slightly right down a lane with stone walls on either side. Cross HIGHER LINCOMBE ROAD and descend on the footpath. Cross another road (right then left) then at the next road turn left and after 50m right.

At the next road turn left, and this time continue to its end, where a footpath leads you into woods. After 100m keep right. The path now zigzags down to the beach. Turn right along the road, and opposite the magnificent Hesketh Crescent (see photo above) turn left up steps (CAR PARK DADDYHOLE PLAIN). The National Coastwatch Institution has a small visitor centre on the Plain.

Now follow the COAST PATH signs. Keep left uphill on a mud path and cross the car park, continuing along the coast path, with various steps and changes of direction, till you reach a T-junction with a broad tarmac path. Turn right past Peaked Tor Cove and cross the rear entrance of the Imperial Hotel – favourite haunt of Hercule Poirot.

Turn left down the road, then bear right along PARKHILL ROAD with its bird's eye view over the harbour. Opposite Vane Hill House turn left down steps which lead to the Strand. Cross the back of the harbour, go through the passage beside the Tourist Information Centre, and you're back at The Pavilion.

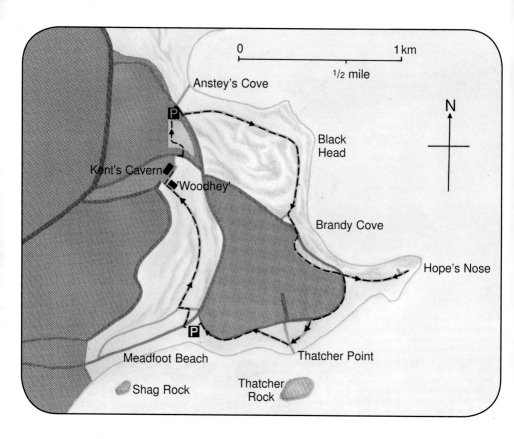

Walk 12 Meadfoot, Kent's Cavern and Ansteys Cove

Distance: 6km (3³/4 miles) – less if you don't go right out to Hope's Nose
Time: 1³/4 hours
Character: An almost rural walk in the middle of a leafy but built-up
area, with delightful woodland and coastal scenery.

Start from the car park at the eastern end of Meadfoot Beach
(SX936633) and head inland, not up the road but up the footpath to
the left of the pumping station. Turn left and immediately right onto
the footpath up the left side of the valley.

Ignore side turnings. The path swings round to the left (KENTS
CAVERN) and begins to climb steeply. Look for a house on the right
called 'Woodhey' and turn right on a narrow and unsigned path
immediately beyond its eagle-topped gateposts, and walk alongside its
boundary wall. This leads into the visitors' car park at Kents Cavern –
a spectacular limestone cave and 'Britain's oldest home'.

Leave the car park at the far right end, down steps, and turn right

down the road, then after 50m turn left, ANSTEYS COVE. Turn left and keep the hedge on your left through a playing field and into the Anstey's Cove car park. (You could if you want descend to the cove, which is very attractive, but you'll need to climb back up again!)

Turn right along the lane for 30m then turn left along the COAST PATH (HOPE'S NOSE) which runs through woodland. Eventually it emerges onto a lane, but just before it does so you should turn left up an unmarked footpath, initially between high walls.

Ultimately there is no avoiding the lane, so turn left along it for a short distance. After 100m turn right up steps then left along a path parallel to the lane. When this rejoins the lane, cross the metal stile opposite.

Walk down to Hope's Nose.

Return to the stile and turn left. Just before a clump of pines, turn left (SOUTH WEST COAST PATH THATCHER POINT). Divert briefly to Thatcher Point, opposite the island, then continue along the coast path back to the road.

Walk down, taking care if there is traffic, back to Meadfoot Beach. An acorn sign on the left indicates steps down to the car park.

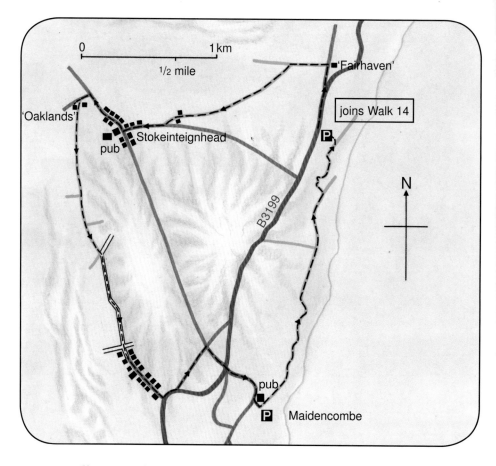

Walk 13   Stokeinteignhead and Maidencombe

Distance: 8 km (5 miles)   Time: 2¾ hours
Character: A very pleasant walk, with views over the Teign estuary and
the coastal cliffs, delightful countryside and a pretty village. It's hilly
country, and there are several steep ascents and descents on the coast
path. After rain you may meet mud or deep puddles, and there are
two short sections on a busy road, 350 m (400 yards) in total. On the
positive side, there are a couple of pubs en route!

Start from the Labrador Bay car park (SX 931704), on the B3199
south of Shaldon. Turn right onto the road (take care!) for 200 m
then bear left up COMMONS LANE. At the top of the hill, opposite
'Fairhaven', turn left onto a track. After 300 m bear left along another
track, which leads down towards Stokeinteignhead.

Join a road into the village. Turn right at the Church House Inn

28

and follow the main street as it wriggles between the cob and thatch cottages. Climb a slope, then turn left at the village approach sign, and immediately bear left onto a track between 'Two Hoots' and 'Oaklands' and head uphill.

The stretch along the ridge does not drain well, so expect puddles.

When the track first divides, keep right and stay on a South South-Easterly course, ignoring side turnings. At length the track surface improves, and later still it turns briefly into a residential street. On reaching the main road, turn left (again, please take great care) and after 100 m turn left down LONGPARK HILL.

At a crossroads turn right up to the main road again. Cross to descend STEEP HILL. At The Thatched Tavern bear left, then in front of a car park, turn left onto the COAST PATH TO SHALDON. Follow the acorn waymarks around properties and then along the cliffs.

At a junction where a path to the right leads downhill, turn left through a gate. Walk ahead to a stile with a faded waymark. Cross the stile and turn right along the well-beaten path along the lower edge of the field, then left up the far side for 100 m, to turn right over another stile. The car park is accessed by a gate on your left, about 100 m into this field.

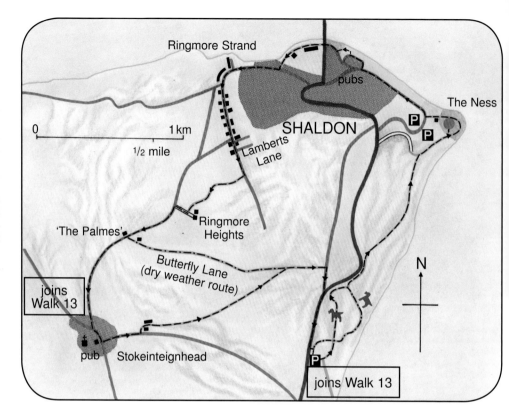

Walk 14 Shaldon

Distance: 7.3 to 9km (4¹/₂ to 5¹/₂ miles)   Time: 2¹/₄ hours
Character: An outstanding walk, with views of coast, estuary and the port/Georgian resort of Teignmouth. Numerous picturesque cottages. There are two steep descents; the climbs are prolonged but gentle.

You could start from the top end of the Ness car park in Shaldon, but I started from the Labrador Bay car park (SX931704). Leave the car park at the vehicle entrance and follow the footpath parallel to the road in the Shaldon direction. This shortly turns right and downhill. After 100m (unless you have a dog) turn left across a stile and follow the path round a field. Cross a stile, then turn left.

(If you have a dog, you should ignore the stile and walk on for 30m. Turn left onto the Coast Path. This adds slightly to the length of the walk and involves an additional steep descent and ascent.)

Climb to the road and turn right. After 90m, take the footpath parallel to the road. When it returns to the road, turn right on COAST

30

PATH SHALDON. Descend steeply. Enter a golf course, keeping to the right. Stay on the path. Keep ahead at COAST PATH SHALDON.

When the path divides, keep right at the yellow arrow and continue to the viewpoint. Turn left and downhill, keeping the fence on your right. Continue down steps and follow the road into Shaldon.

There are several routes through the village to the bridge. I followed the beach, then RIVERSIDE, briefly along the foreshore and back onto a street. At the bridge, cross the main road and follow the riverside walk.

Reaching a road, turn right and continue till it bends inland, then turn left up HIGHER RINGMORE ROAD, passing many thatched cottages. Ignore side turnings. Some 200 m after Ringmore Farm, turn right up a track, which snakes uphill.

Reaching a house drive, turn right down to a lane. Turn left. In dry weather you can turn left opposite 'The Palmes' up an unmarked track, actually called 'Butterfly Lane', which is a pleasant short-cut. But after wet weather it can be impassable without wading through deep puddles, so it is prudent to continue along the lane into Stokeinteignhead.

Keep left, then turn left opposite the Church House pub. After 300 m bear left up a track (dead end sign) and past a barn, then climb steadily uphill. At a junction of tracks turn right, uphill. Reaching a lane near a trig. point, turn right down to the main road. Continue along it with great care for 200 m, then turn left 20 m short of the vehicle entrance to the car park.

Some other Bossiney walks books

Fairly easy walks on Dartmoor (3-9 km walks)
Shortish walks on Dartmoor (5-8 km walks)
Shortish walks in East Devon (5-10 km walks)
Shortish walks near Exeter (4-9 km walks)
Shortish walks: the South Devon Coast (5-8 km walks)
Really short walks: the South Devon Coast (3-5 km walks)
Ten town trails – South Devon
Dartmoor pub walks (7-14 km walks)
Walks on High Dartmoor (7-20 km walks)

Some Bossiney guide books

The Devon Beach and Cove Guide
High Dartmoor – a Shortish Guide
Dartmouth – a Shortish Guide
Exeter – a Shortish Guide
The South Hams – a Shortish Guide

For a full list of our books see www.bossineybooks.com